CW00429744

Gibraltar
United Kingdom

City Map

🌐 Glob:us

Gibraltar, United Kingdom — City Map
By Jason Patrick Bates

First Edition: October 2017

Scale / 1:4000

| 50m

| 500ft

Map Overview

Map Symbols

▬	Highway	◉	Map continuation page
▬	Street	····	Path

🏆	Archaeological site	🔳	Kiosk
i	Artwork	✕	Level crossing
🏧	Atm	📖	Library
Y	Bar	🗼	Lighthouse
🚲	Bicycle rental	🏛	Memorial
🍺	Biergarten	🔲	Memorial plaque
☸	Buddhist temple	1	Monument
🚌	Bus station	🏛	Museum
🚏	Bus stop	☪	Muslim mosque
☕	Cafe	🏙	Neighbourhood
⛺	Camping site	🎵	Nightclub
🚗	Car rental	P	Parking
◠	Cave entrance	▲	Peak
🏔	Chalet	💊	Pharmacy
🔌	Charging station	🎋	Picnic site
†	Church / Monastery	🛝	Playground
🎬	Cinema	👮	Police
⚖	Courthouse	✉	Post office
🏬	Department store	🏤	Prison
🐾	Dog park	🍺	Pub
🚰	Drinking water	🚆	Railway
🧴	Dry cleaning	🍴	Restaurant
⬍	Elevator	⛩	Shinto temple
⚑	Embassy	☬	Sikh temple
🍔	Fast food	🏃	Sports centre
⚓	Ferry terminal	🛒	Supermarket
🔥	Fire station	☯	Taoist temple
⛲	Fountain	🚕	Taxi
⛽	Fuel	📞	Telephone
⛳	Golf course	🎭	Theatre
🏨	Guest house	🚻	Toilets
🕉	Hindu temple	🏛	Townhall
✚	Hospital	⚟	Traffic signals
🏢	Hostel	❋	Viewpoint
🛏	Hotel	🛝	Water park
i	Information	⛺	Wilderness hut
✡	Jewish synagogue	✗	Windmill

4 Área de autocaravanas

P

W
B

Victoria Stadium   Victoria S

10

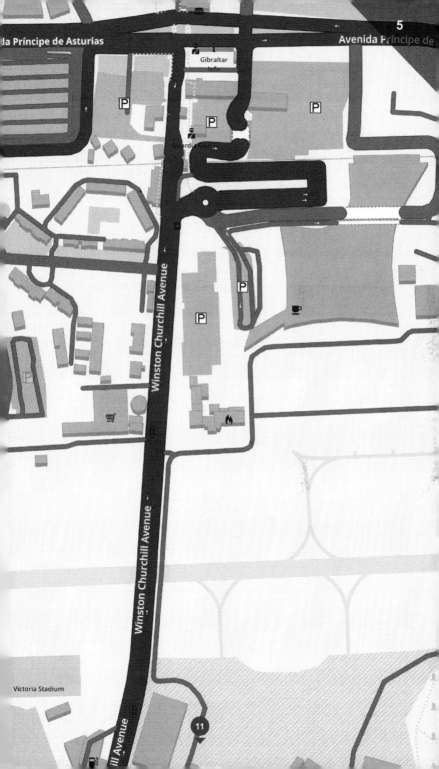

turias

P

Antena Repetidora
TV

12

13

Mons Calpe Road

⚓
Cruise Liner
terminal

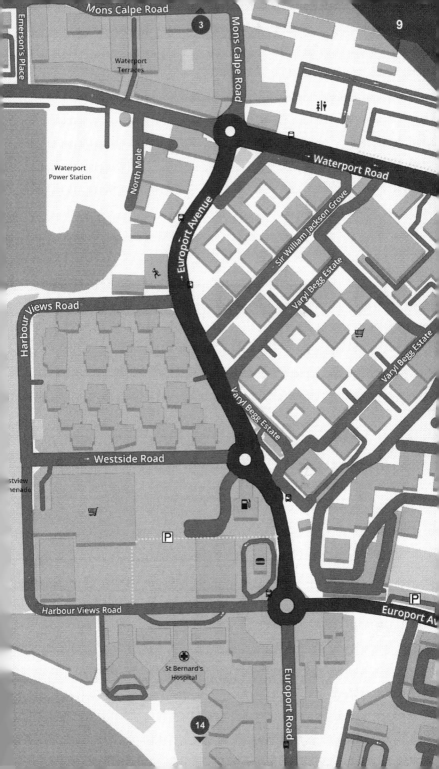

4

Victoria

Bayside Road

St. Ar

Glacis Road

Admiral's Walk

Waterport Road

Ocean Village

Smith Dorrien A

Corral Road

Queensway

Gibraltar
Public Market

Casemates
Square

Crutchetts Ramp

Road to the Lines

Fishmarket Lane

Line Wall Road

Queensway

Costa Lane

Turnbulls Lane

Castle Road

Lower Castle

Castle Ramp

American
War Memorial

Parliament Lane

Engineer Lane

nue

clamation Road

Irish Town

Tuckey's Lane

15

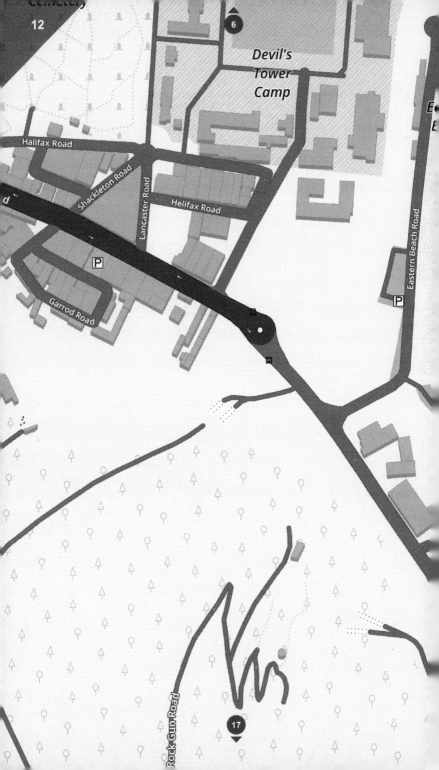

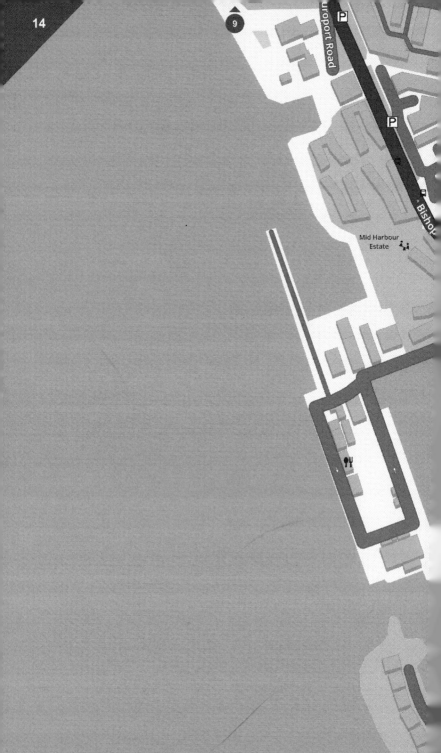

9

roport Road

Bishop

Mid Harbour
Estate

The Islan

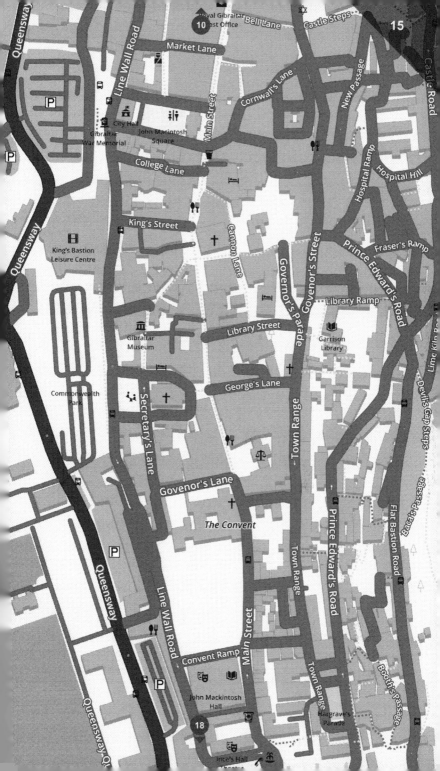

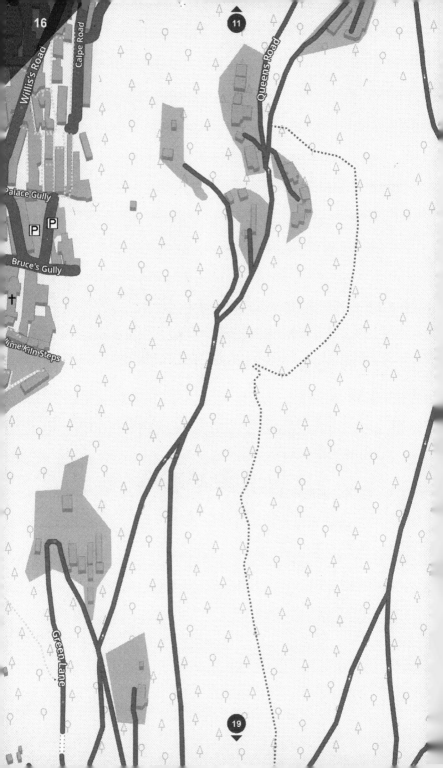

Willis's Road

Calpe Road

Queens Road

11

Palace Gully

P   P

Bruce's Gully

†

Lime Kiln Steps

Green Lane

19

Sir Herbert Road

Catalan Bay Road

P

Catalan
Bay

CATALAN BAY

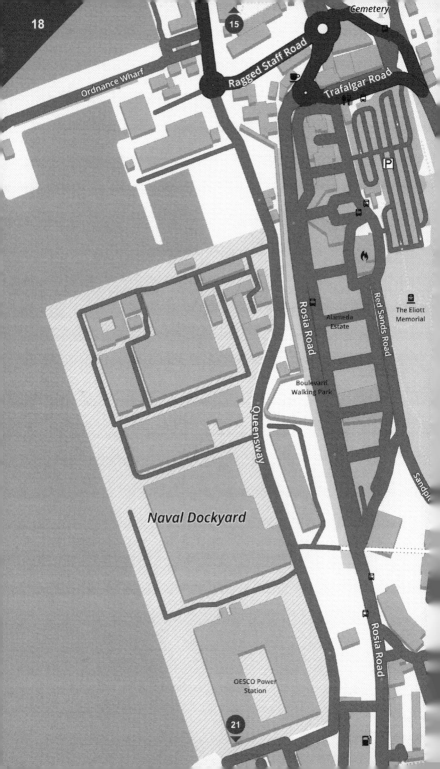

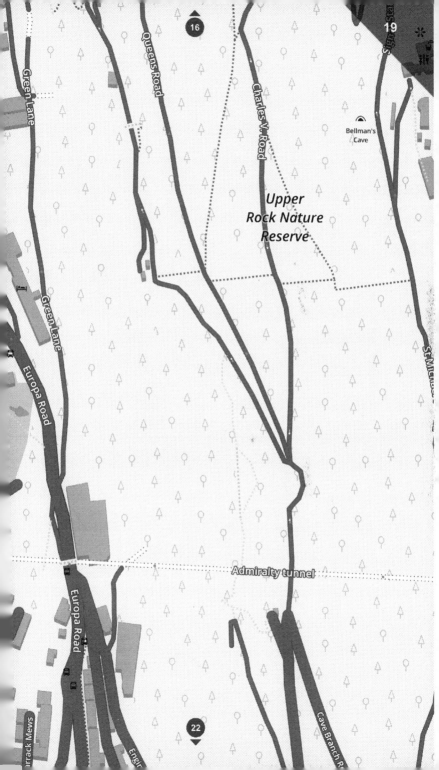

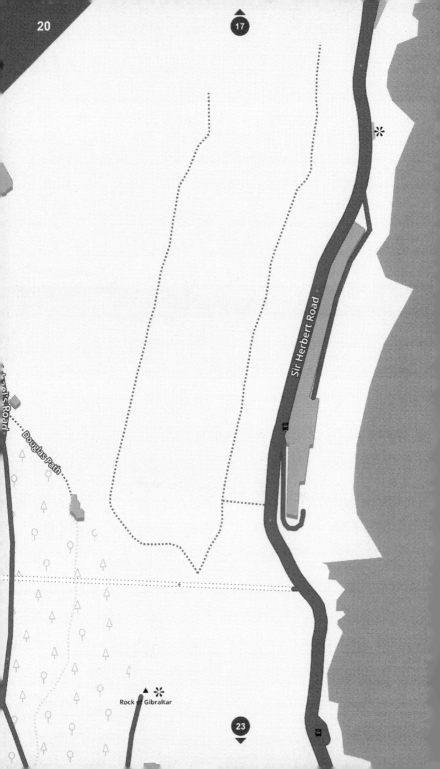

17

Sir Herbert Road

Trails Road

Douglas Path

Rock of Gibraltar

23

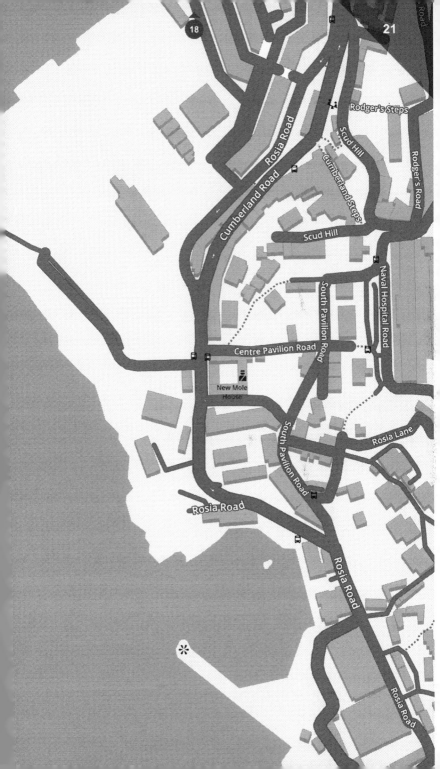

South Barrack Road

19

Naval Hospital Road

Mount Road

Mount Road

Engineer Road

Buena Vista Road

Ellerton R

24

l Hospital

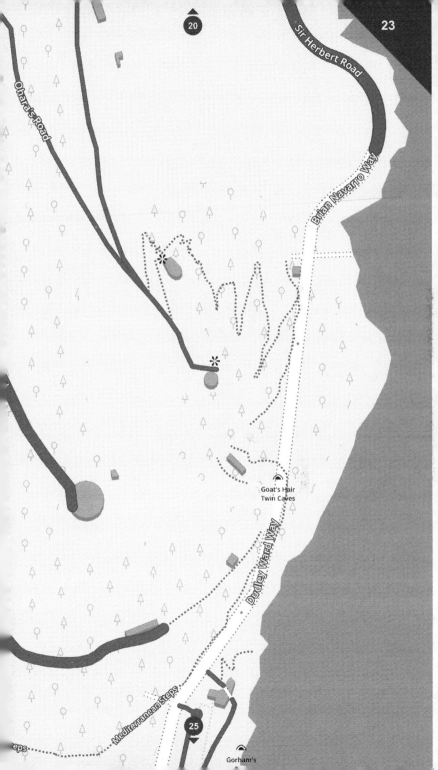

O'hara's Road

Sir Herbert Road

Brian Navarro Way

Dudley Ward Way

Goat's Hair
Twin Caves

Mediterranean Steps

eps

Gorham's

20

25

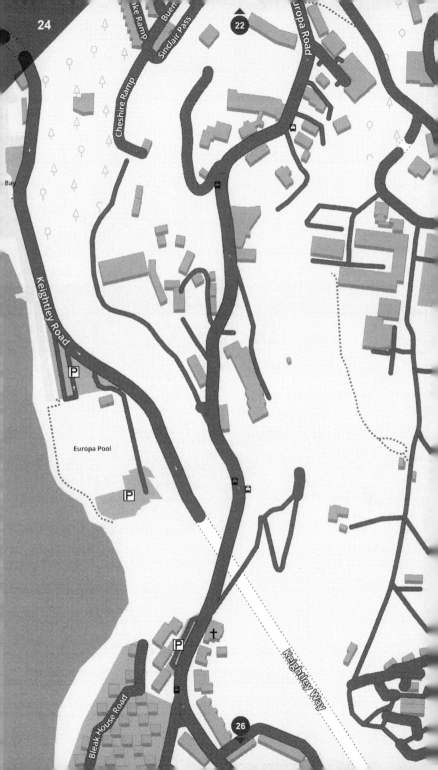

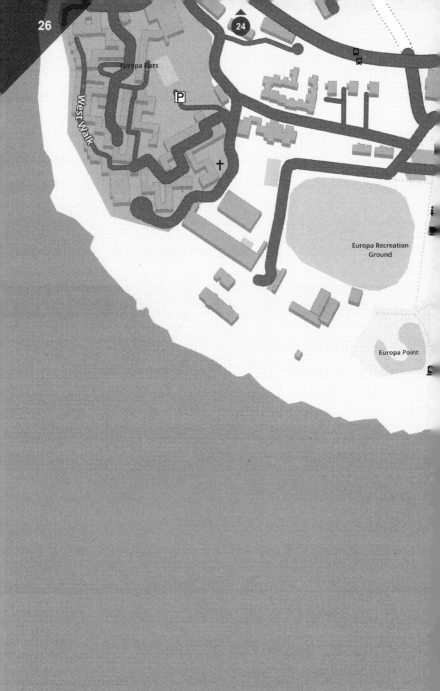

24

Europa Flats

West Walk

P

✝

Europa Recreation
Ground

Europa Point

Streets

A

Abecasis passage 15
Admiral's walk 4, 10
Admiralty tunnel . 18, 20
Ansaldo's passage 10, 15
Arengo's palace lane . 16
Armstrong's steps 18
Arow street 23
Ashbourne ramp 22
Avenida 20 de abril 5
Avenida principe de
    asturias 4–7

B

Baca's passage 15
Bado's passage 15
Baker's passage 15
Bay access road . . 12, 13
Bayside road 10, 11
Bedlam court 10
Bell lane 15
Benoliel's passage . . . 15
Benzimra's alley 15
Biship rapallo's ramp . 15
Bishop caruana road . 14,
    15
Bleak house road 24, 26
Bomb house lane 15
Booth's passage 15
Boschetti's steps 15
Boyd street 18
Brian navarro way 23
Bruce's gully 15, 16
Buena vista road . 22, 24

C

Calle gibraltar 5, 6
Calpe road 11, 16
Cannon lane 15

Carrera's passage 10
Casemates square . . . 10
Casemates squere . . . 10
Castle ramp 10, 15
Castle road 10, 15, 16
Castle steps . . . 11, 15, 16
Catalan bay road 17
Cathedral square 15
Cave branch road . 19, 22
Centre pavilion road . . 21
Charles v ramp 15
Charles v. road . . . 16, 19
Cheshire ramp 24
Chicardo's passage . . 15
Chichester ramp . . 22, 24
City mill lane 15
College lane 15
Convent place 15
Convent ramp 15
Cooperage lane 10
Cornwall's lane 15
Cornwall's parade 15
Corral road 10
Costa lane 10
Costa ramp 10
Crutchetts ramp 10
Cumberland road 21
Cumberland steps . . . 21

D

Danino's ramp 16
Demaya's ramp 10
Devil's gap footpath . 15,
    16
Devil's gap steps 15
Devil's tongue road . . 10
Devil's tower road . 11, 12
Dobinson way 25
Douglas path 20
Drinkwater road 11
Dudley ward way . 23, 25

E

East walk 26
Eastern beach road . . 12
Eaton industrial park . 11
Eliott's way 18
Eliotts way 18
Ellerton ramp 22, 24
Emerson's place 9
Engineer lane 10
Engineer road 19, 22
Europa advance road 25,
    27
Europa road . . . 15, 18, 19,
    22, 24, 26, 27
Europort avenue . . . 9, 10
Europort road 9, 14

F

Fishmarket lane 10
Flat bastion road 15
Forbes road 11
Forty steps 15
Fraser's ramp 15

G

Gardiner's road 15, 18, 19
Garrod road 12
Gavino's court 15
Gavino's passage 15
George's lane 15
Giro's passage 15
Glacis road 10, 11
Govenor's lane 15
Govenor's street 15
Governor's parade . . . 15
Gowland's ramp 15
Green lane 16, 19

H

Halifax road 11, 12
Harbour views road . . . 9
Hargrave's court 15
Hargrave's parade 15
Hargrave's ramp 15
Heaton road 11
Helifax road 12
Horse barrack court . . 15
Horse barrack lane . . . 15
Hospital hill 15
Hospital ramp 15
Hospital steps 15
Hugo road 11

I

Irish place 10
Irish town 10, 15

J

Jasmine's ramp 10
John macintosh square
    15
Johnstone's passage . 15

K

Kavanagh's court 15
Keightley road 24, 26
Keightley way 24, 26
King's street 15
King's yard lane 15

L

Lake ramp 24
Lancaster road 12
Landport tunnel 10
Library gardens 15
Library ramp 15
Library street 15
Lime kiln road 15, 16
Lime kiln steps . . . 15, 16
Line wall road . 10, 15, 18
Lopez's ramp 15, 16
Lower castle road 10, 15
Lynch's lane 10

M

Main street 10, 15
Market lane 15

Mcphail's passage . . . 15
Mediterranean road . 22, 23
Mediterranean steps 22, 23
Mess house lane 15
Mons calpe road 8, 9
Morello's ramp 15
Mount road 22

N

Naval hospital hill 22, 24
Naval hospital road . . 21, 22
New passage 15
New street 15
North mole 8, 9

O

Ocean village 10
Ocean village prome-
    nade 10
Ohara's road 20, 23
Old brympton close . . 22
Ordnance wharf 18

P

Palace gully 16
Paradise ramp 15, 16
Parliament lane 10
Parody's passage 10
Paseo maritimo
    poniente 4
Paseo maritimo de
    poniente 4
Pezzi's steps 15
Pitman's alley 15
Police barrack's lane . 15
Prince edward's road . 15

Q

Queen's lane 15
Queens road . . . 11, 16, 19
Queensway . . . 10, 15, 18
Queensway quay . 15, 18

R

Ragged staff road 18
Reclamation road . 10, 15
Red sands road 18

Richardson's passage
    10, 11, 15, 16
Road to the lines 10
Rock gun road . 12, 16, 17
Rodger's road 21
Rodger's steps 21
Rosia dale 21, 22
Rosia lane 21
Rosia road 18, 21
Royal anglian way 19

S

Sandpits 18
Scud hill 21
Scud hill steps 21
Secretary's lane 15
Serfaty's passage 10
Shackleton road 12
Shakery's passage . . . 15
Shrine walk 26
Signal station road 11, 16, 19
Sinclair pass 22, 24
Sir herbert road . . . 12, 17, 20, 23
Sir william jackson
    grove 9
Smith dorrien avenue 10
Sortie road 11
South barrack mews 19, 22
South barrack ramp . 21, 22
South barrack road . . 19, 22
South pavilion court . . 21
South pavilion road . . . 21
South pavilion steps . . 21
South shed's place . . . 21
Spur battery road 22, 23
St michael's road 19, 20, 22
St. anne's road 10, 11
Sunnyside steps 22
Sunset close 22, 24

T

Tank ramp 10, 11
Tankerville road 11
Tarik road 10, 11, 15
The boardwalk,
    tradewinds 10
The island street . . 14, 18
Tigge road 11
Town range 15

Points of Interest

...

100 Ton Gun 👤 21

A

Alameda Gardens and
Open Air Theatre
👤 18
American War Memo-
rial 👤 10
Apes' Den 👤 19

B

Bellman's Cave 👤 19
Breakneck battery 👤 20
Buena vista barracks
and battery 👤 . . . 24

C

Casemates Police Sta-
tion i 10
Casemates Square 👤 10
Cross Of Sacrifice 👤 . . 11
Cruise Line Terinal ⚓ 8

D

Devil's gap battery.1902
👤 16
Duke of Wellington
Monument 👤 . . . 18

E

Europa Flats 🏢 . . . 24, 26
Europa Point Light-
house 👤 27

G

Gibraltar Airport i . . 4–6
Gibraltar Marina ⚓ . . . 10
Gibraltar Museum 🏛 . 15
Goat's Hair Twin Caves
👤 23
Gorham's Cave 👤 23
Great siege tunnels 👤12

H

Harding's Battery 👤 . . 26

M

Market Place Terminus
🚌 10
Moorish castle 👤 11

N

Napier of magdala bat-
tery 👤 21
New mole house 🛥 . . 21
Nun's Well 👤 26

P

Princess Caroline Bat-
tery 👤 11

R

Rock of Gibraltar 👤 . . 20

S

Saint Bernard's Hospital
✚ 9
St Michael's Cave 👤 . . 22

T

The Convent 👤 15
Tourist Information Of-
fice i 26
Tourist Office i 5
Town Hall 👤 15

V

Victoria Stadium 🏃 . 5, 11

W

War Memorial 👤 15
World war ii tunnels 👤
11

Printed in Great Britain
by Amazon

70620924R00023